Interactive Storytelling Ideas for Teachers

Jane Elling Haas

Illustrated by
Carolyn Braun

CPH™
SAINT LOUIS

To my parents, Alfred and Virginia Elling,

who first taught me about Jesus' love and forgiveness

and continue to do so through their Christian words and actions.

I thank God for His blessings to them—

their faith-living and faith-sharing, and

their creative and nurturing qualities, of which they freely give.

Unless otherwise stated, Scripture quotations taken from THE HOLY BIBLE, NEW INTERNATIONAL VERSION®. Copyright © 1973, 1978, 1984 by the International Bible Society. Used by permission of Zondervan Publishing House. All rights reserved.

The "NIV" and "New International Version" trademarks are registered in the United States Patent and Trademark Office by the International Bible Society. Use of either trademark requires the permission of the International Bible Society.

Scripture quotations marked TEV are from the Good News Bible, the Bible in TODAY'S ENGLISH VERSION. Copyright © American Bible Society, 1966, 1971, 1976. Used by permission.

Copyright © 1995 Concordia Publishing House
3558 S. Jefferson Avenue, St. Louis, MO 63118-3968
Manufactured in the United States of America

1 2 3 4 5 6 7 8 9 10   04 03 02 01 00 99 98 97 96 95

Contents

Introduction

❑ What Is Storytelling?

For centuries people have told stories about family members and events and have passed down special teachings from one generation to another. Our Lord Jesus was the Master Storyteller. While He lived on earth, He gathered people wherever He went to tell them of the heavenly Father's love, illustrating principles and commandments with anecdotes and stories in order to teach people. We call these teaching stories *parables,* earthly stories that have a heavenly meaning.

Telling stories to one another is the most common and most effective way of communicating ideas. Telling the chronological facts of an event in an interesting, appealing way is simple and easy for some, but complicated and difficult for others.

Our goal is to learn more about storytelling, the skills a good storyteller acquires and uses, different methods of telling the same story, and ways to enhance storytelling with visual aids. Stories in words and dimensional objects have a lasting effect on the listeners.

As Christian leaders we have an important impact on children and adults of all ages when we tell a story effectively. In our roles, there are times for sharing with large groups, small groups, and individuals. In each situation, we have an opportunity to share the Good News of God's saving love for us through Jesus. In each situation, we can tell stories.

By telling stories of Jesus' loving actions for all people, we share God's love, communicate the Gospel as Jesus commanded (Matthew 28:19), and actively live our faith.

❑ Goals of a Storyteller

O my people, hear my teaching;
   listen to the words of my mouth.
I will open my mouth in parables,
   I will utter hidden things, things from
      of old—
what we have heard and known,
   what our fathers have told us.
We will not hide them from their children;
   we will tell the next generation
the praiseworthy deeds of the Lord,
   His power, and the wonders He has
      done.
He decreed statutes for Jacob
   and established the law in Israel,
which He commanded our forefathers
   to teach their children,
so the next generation would know them,
   even the children yet to be born,
   and they in turn would tell their
      children.
Then they would put their trust in God
   and would not forget His deeds
   but would keep his commands.

                              Psalm 78:1–7

As we tell the stories God has given us in His Word, we will

- identify with the story we want to tell. We'll tell of God our Creator's love and care, of Jesus' love and forgiveness through His saving action, of the Holy Spirit's work in our hearts to keep us in faith.

- confess and witness to our Christian faith as we visualize what we want to tell our listeners.

- share stories that are important to us. Storytelling is a shared experience through which we develop and build relationships with our listeners, while creating a common tradition.

- share Christian values. At a level far deeper than just words, storytelling helps us communicate values and truths to our listeners that, through the power of the Holy Spirit, help them grow in faith.

❏ Prepare to Storytell—Practice for Better Storytelling

Be yourself. Those are the best words of advice to a storyteller. God has graciously given us a variety of gifts to use in order to further His kingdom. Reflect on the gifts God has given you. In prayer, ask God to show you the areas in which you have the strength to do His work. Jot them down on paper. Thank God for His gifts and for His help as you serve Him. Ask Him to help you communicate His Word clearly through storytelling.

Remember that the story you are about to tell must be real. When it becomes real in your mind and heart, then you can make it real to the audience.

- Before telling a story, pray that the Holy Spirit will help you speak clearly, relate your words appropriately to the listeners, and effectively communicate your message.

- Discern the central message of the Bible story. What is God's action in this story? How did God show His love or care for the people? What did God do then and what does He do today for you and me? Emphasize the Gospel truth from each Bible story rather than the facts. Include a balance of Law and Gospel in your teaching. We can't keep God's Law perfectly as He commands. That knowledge confronts us and opens us to the refreshment of the Gospel—Jesus kept the Law perfectly for us and died in our stead. Storytell in order to plant seeds of faith and to help them grow. Storytell to help a student's relationship with Jesus Christ develop and strengthen.

- Become so familiar with the story that it becomes part of you. Read and review it ahead of time repeatedly. Practice telling the story to a family member, a friend, or to yourself by using a mirror and an audio- or a videocassette recorder. Practice manipulating the visual helps. Practice, practice, practice.

- Speak clearly. Read aloud directly from the Bible. Tell a Bible story naturally. Make sure you can pronounce names and present the events in the correct sequence. Tell the Bible story as God tells it in His Word without embellishing and creating extravagant details.

- Know the story so well that you can maintain eye contact with your students. Listeners will be good listeners if they see you looking at them rather than at a book or at a guide.

- Vary the pitch, tone, and volume of your voice. As you review a story, decide which parts need solemn, quiet whisperlike expressions, and which parts require excited, loud, vocal expressions.

- Make the Bible story come alive by relating it to the lives of your students.

For example, talk about how happy and thankful they are when a family member or a friend gets well. Relate those feelings to those of the official when Jesus healed his son. Applications help your students relate Jesus' teachings to their lives.

- Use visual words. Nouns and verbs usually work best. Too many adjectives can clutter the description. For example, it is interesting for the middle-grade listener to imagine the scene as you say, "David took off the heavy coat of armor and big bronze helmet. 'I cannot go in these, because I'm not used to wearing such big and heavy equipment,' he told King Saul. So David took his wooden staff, put five smooth stones in his leather shepherd's pouch, and carried his homemade sling as he approached the large Philistine, Goliath" (1 Samuel 17:39–40).

- Use auditory words. When you tell about God delivering the city of Jericho into Joshua's hands, use words such as "march," "blow the trumpets," and "give a loud shout" (Joshua 6). Have the children roleplay the words at the appropriate times in the story. Have them use trumpets, rhythm instruments, and kazoos.

- Bridge the love, care, and salvation God showed His people long ago to the everyday lives of the students. For example, just as God took care of His helper Paul as he traveled and told people about God's love and forgiveness, so God watches over you and keeps you in His loving care. He helps you, too, as you travel away from your homes. God keeps you safe, just as He kept Paul safe when the ship wrecked and the soldiers

wanted to kill him. God still had work Paul to do. God has work for you to do and He helps you too (Acts 27–28).

- Let students be active participants. Have them finish a sentence. They might ring bells every time they hear you say "angels." Have them move clothespin characters or tube people as they roleplay the story. Ask them to pull surprise objects from a bag, a box, or pockets in your skirt or shirt and hold them as the story progresses. Have young listeners echo short story sentences. Have them help set simple story sentences to a familiar melody and sing the story together as a class. Ask middle- and upper-grade students to help prepare, show, and save the visual objects suggested in this book. Some might create their own visual helps—puppets, booklets, audio- and videocassettes, costumes, and props—to later review and retell the Bible story for another class.

Your face, voice, eyes, and body movements demonstrate your interest and enthusiasm. Sometimes visuals and other helps are not needed. Show and tell the story in your words and actions. A visual item can help to reinforce the words and concepts you present.

❏ Age-Appropriate Storytelling Hints

A two-year-old might give you only two minutes of attention. That's typical. Tell very short Bible stories to very young children. Gauge the length of your story to the age of the audience. The hard part is condensing a Bible story into four minutes for four-year-olds or five minutes for five-year-olds. Just tell the highlights of a Bible story to very young children. As they grow older, details can be added. Emphasize what you want remembered in simple words: God's love, care, and protection; forgiveness; the Gospel; the cross, and Jesus' saving grace.

By showing students a related object, you can help them make a *connection* between the hearing, seeing, feeling, and doing. Even two-year-olds, when shown a wooden cross on Sunday morning, will often recognize crosses during the week. They see the cross shape on walls, within signs, as telephone poles, in furniture, and in toys. As they paint, roll play dough, make sponge prints, and draw cross shapes on their own, young children recreate the cross and are reminded of what Jesus has done for them in His death and resurrection.

Very young children (ages 1 through 3) like to hear brief, simple Bible stories about Jesus in short sentences. They can begin to develop an attitude of joyful praise and thanks to Jesus for His friendship, for His coming as a little baby to be their Savior (though they don't understand *Savior* yet), and His care for them and their families. They don't need explanations or backgrounds of biblical people and events. Do explain words such as *manger*, *friend*, and *family* as you use them. *Show* them objects to help them connect your *words* to a *concrete thing*.

Prekindergarten children (ages 4 and 5) like to hear brief Bible stories in short sentences. They enjoy hearing a big, important word and learning its meaning in the context of the story. For example, "Jesus' helpers in the boat were terrified! They were afraid of the stormy wind and lightning." Prekindergartners enjoy echo-ing short story sentences, supplying a missing word, singing simple Bible story words to familiar piggyback tunes, and illustrating Bible stories with their own pictures.

Kindergarten and primary level children (ages 6 through 8) like to hear Bible stories with a few challenging words they can help define. They enjoy keeping word books. Have one student print the special word, and ask another student to draw a picture to explain it. Stories should be no more than six or seven minutes long in order to keep their attention. They also like to review a Bible story by writing and illustrating the stories in booklets for the classroom. You can also have the students paint a story mural as a review activity.

Junior level students (ages 9 and 10) are usually able to listen to a longer Bible story up to about 10–12 minutes. They will understand the roles of the characters and the sequence of events. Often they are able to retell the Bible story from the previous week. This group thoroughly enjoys roleplaying to review and retell Bible stories. These students are good at creating visual items, such as tube puppets, paper-bag characters, craft-stick people, and dioramas, and using them to share Bible stories with younger children.

A storyteller will keep the interest and attention of **preteen level students (ages 11 and 12)** by being very well-prepared, correlating the Bible story truths with real events in the students' lives, and involving the students through the use of visual helps. Encourage the students to help make storytelling visuals. They are creative and like to be in charge of special projects. Challenge them to help take care of God's world by saving household items to recycle into storytelling objects.

It's extra challenging to tell Bible stories to **junior high students (ages 13 and 14).** Many have heard or have read the Bible story before, and it isn't cool to want to hear it again. Tell the Bible story, or have read it directly from the Bible. You might have the students follow along in their own Bibles as you read aloud. (Reading aloud to junior, preteen, and junior high students is an excellent way to model good reading and language skills.) Spend the majority of your 10–15 storytelling minutes relating the Bible story and its truths to a situation or an event close to your students' experience. Let them practice the art of storytelling in small groups. Have them draw Bible stories from a basket, practice telling them, make their own visuals, and present their stories to younger children.

❏ Helps in This Book

You'll find simple line drawings of Bible characters, objects, and teaching tools to create special visuals for storytelling. Practice and adapt ideas to fit the needs of your students. Remember to involve them in preparing visuals, completing illustrations during storytelling, and using the dimensional helps to review Bible stories.

God, our Father, has written the stories in the Bible for us to read, learn, and share. The key ingredients, the very best stories, are here for us already. We need not create them. We need not embellish them. We need only to *tell* them.

Through a storyteller's imagination, each Bible story comes to life and seems real to the listener as he/she hears God's Word, watches objects give concrete relationships and action to the story, and leaves with a better understanding of what God's Word means in his/her life today.

I pray that you will enjoy becoming a good storyteller/illustrator as you use your gifts and a variety of dimensional objects to glorify God and plant seeds of His Word in the hearts of many listeners.

God Made Our Beautiful World

Genesis 1:1–2:3

Bible words: [God] has made everything beautiful. *Ecclesiastes 3:11*

A Creation Tree

As you tell the story of creation to young children (those in nursery, kindergarten, and primary grades), do not be concerned about the numerical day on which God created specific things. Emphasize God's wonderful creation and His happiness with His beautiful world, of which we are a part. Older students enjoy the challenge of categorizing each day's creations and remembering this sequence.

Before storytelling time, place a tree branch in an empty two-pound coffee can. Fill the can with stones and sand or plaster of Paris. Prepare visuals to hang on the creation tree as you tell about God's creations on each day. Use yarn or ribbon to hang the objects.

Possible objects include: a plastic globe to represent the earth; a square of white or yellow construction paper; a square of black construction paper; cotton batting for clouds; a sealed tube of water; a sealed tube of earth; vegetable and fruit seed packets; magazine pictures or photos of beautiful trees; a sun-catcher; a white whiffle ball to represent the moon; a square of dark blue construction paper with star stickers; a variety of colorful birds (from a craft store);

plastic sea creatures and fish; plastic land animals and reptiles; dolls to represent a man and a woman; and a happy face to represent God, who was pleased with His creation. He blessed the seventh day and made it holy, and then He rested.

As a review, have your students retell the story in their own words while hanging the visuals on the creation tree. Older students enjoy putting the days of creation in sequential order. Supply them with poster board or art paper so they can make their own "creation booklets" as a review.

Emphasize to your students that everything God made was good. Our Creator made every part of His world beautiful and special, including you and me. And He continues to take good care of His world.

Tree Branch

Plaster of Paris
Stones

Two-pound coffee can

11

The Fall into Sin/ God Promises a Savior

Genesis 2:8–3:24

Bible words: [Jesus] will save His people from their sins. *Matthew 1:21*

Sand Pan Garden

Fill a large container half full of sand. The under-the-bed storage box by Rubbermaid works well. It also has a tightly fitting lid for easy storage.

Gather twigs and greenery to represent trees and bushes and arrange them in the sand. You also can use silk or plastic greenery and small flowers to create a Garden of Eden scene. Place one green tree in the middle of the garden to represent the tree of life and another tree to represent the tree of the knowledge of good and evil.

To represent Adam, place a plastic figure of a man in the garden. As you storytell, print the name *Adam* on the chalkboard or newsprint using uppercase and lowercase letters. This helps students visualize his name. Place different kinds of plastic animals around Adam. Place birds in the trees and on the ground. Then place a plastic figure of a woman beside Adam. Print the word *woman* in uppercase and lowercase letters.

Rubbermaid container

Add a plastic snake near Adam and Eve. Or you can roll clay or play dough into a snake and coil it in the tree.

Add a piece of fruit (such as a peach, an apple, or an orange) to the tree of the knowledge of good and evil. Form the small fruit shape from colored play dough or clay.

Move the fruit into Eve's hand. Then move it into Adam's hand to signify that they both ate the fruit from the forbidden tree.

As you tell about the shame they felt after disobeying God, move Adam and Eve behind the tallest trees and bushes.

Print the name *Eve* beside the word *woman*. Draw sad faces on the chalkboard beside both names.

Move Adam and Eve outside the garden. Attach pieces of fabric to the plastic figures with tape to represent the clothing they needed after they disobeyed God.

Place a large cross between Adam and Eve. Use a cross from your home or make a simple one from craft sticks or twigs.

Cut out a big red heart from construction paper. Print *Jesus* on the heart as you tell how God promised a Savior for all people. This Savior is Jesus, who came to die for everyone's sins and then rose from the dead to win the victory over sin, death, and the devil. Attach the heart to the cross with tape or craft glue.

God kept His promise. He still loved Adam and Eve and cared for them. Many years later, God sent His Son, Jesus, to die for their sins and for the sins of the whole world. Draw smiling faces beside their names on the chalkboard.

God sent Jesus for you and me. He loves us and He forgives us. That's why we're so thankful and happy! Give each student a happy face sticker to wear.

God Saves Noah and His Family

Genesis 6:1–9:17

Bible words: [God says,] "I will save my people." *Zechariah 8:7*

Skirt Pocket Surprises

Before class, sew a full skirt from a colorful fabric. Sew many pockets onto the skirt using a variety of fabric designs and colors. (You also can make a shirt with many pockets.)

Place an object in each pocket before you begin storytelling. Include a plastic figure to represent Noah. If possible, draw a heart with a cross inside and glue it to the Noah figure to represent his faithfulness to the Lord.

In other pockets place plastic figures to represent Noah's wife, his three sons, and their wives. Remove these figures from the pockets as you tell how God kept them safe inside the ark.

Place a plastic boat in another pocket to represent the ark. Explain that God told Noah and his sons to build a very, very big ark. Compare the size of the ark to a boat "bigger than our school (or church)."

In another pocket, have a rainbow suncatcher. Bring it out as you tell about God's promise to Noah.

For the lesson application, pull a large red heart with a cross drawn inside it from another pocket. Remind the students that we can trust God to keep His promises to us too. We thank Him for His love and care and for sending Jesus to be our Savior.

Noah Noah's wife

Plastic boat

Rainbow suncatcher

The Tower of Babel

Genesis 11:1–9

Bible words: I am the Lord, your God, … have no other gods before me. *Deuteronomy 5:6–7*

Build a Tower

Cover shoe boxes, cereal boxes, and tissue boxes with red and orange construction paper to represent bricks. Cut strips of black construction paper or black felt (or another fabric) to represent the tar.

Ask one or two students to help you tell this Bible story in the first person. Build the tower, block by block, as you speak.

Let's make bricks.
Okay. Let's do!
What a good idea!

We'll need to use this clay since we don't have any stone.
Stone is hard to find in this country.
We can mold the clay like this.
Then we'll bake the brick shapes until they are very hard.

We can use all these baked brick shapes to build a tower!
Come, let's build a city for ourselves.
Let's build a tower that reaches to the heavens!
Let's make a city we can live in so we'll always be together.

We'll make a name for ourselves.
We'll be famous!

(Begin to speak in nonsense syllables.)

Sa no mini cha zee.
Woo vu tra?
Fro maka zonu ba.

Emphasize that God confused the people's words as they spoke so that they wouldn't understand each other. He did this because they acted proud and thought they did not need God. Without a common language, they couldn't work together or get anything done. God scattered these people all over the earth, and they had to stop building their city.

God wants us to put Him first. That is His First Commandment to us. He promises that when we keep Him at the center of our lives, He will bless us and always be with us. When we forget to praise and worship God as our Creator and Savior, when we think we can do everything ourselves, we can't see the cross of Christ and the hope it offers. In His mercy, God forgives us when we repent of our sins. He offers forgiveness and His continuing loving care. We rejoice that we are God's children and that He daily takes care of us.

Black felt for tar

The Lord Appears to Abraham

Genesis 18:1–19

Bible words: The Lord has kept the promise He made. *1 Kings 8:20*

Visitors to the Tent

Before you begin telling this Bible story, set up a small tent in an area of your classroom. Narrate the story or ask another teacher to narrate. If you narrate the story, ask three additional people (adults or youth) to play the parts of the three visitors to Abraham's tent—the Lord God and the two angels. Ask a woman to play Sarah. Have a dishpan with a little water in it, a towel, a loaf of bread, and a small container of yogurt or cottage cheese for use as props.

Tell the story as Abraham. Begin the Bible story sitting at the entrance to the tent. Tell the Bible story as you run to meet the three visitors, wash their feet, and dry them with the towel. Offer them a place to rest and eat.

Continue the roleplay with the departure of the visitors. The individual playing the Lord should speak the Lord's promise to bless Abraham and keep His promises to him.

What were some of God's blessings to Abraham and his family? God certainly took good care of them!

What blessings from God are the same for us today as they were for Abraham? He certainly takes good care of us!

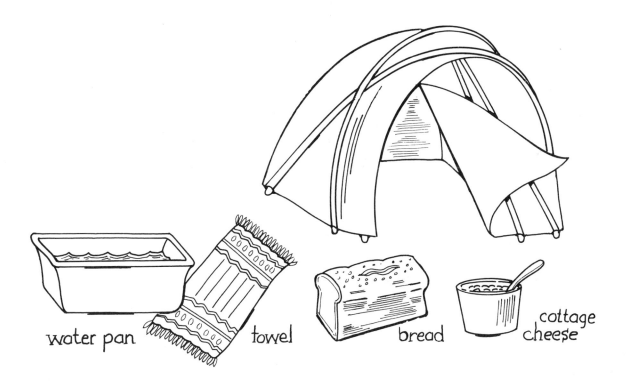

water pan   towel   bread   cottage cheese

God Helps Joseph Forgive His Brothers

Genesis 44–45

Bible words: Forgive as the Lord forgave you. *Colossians 3:13*

A Silver Cup in a Sack

Tell this Bible story from Joseph's perspective. Have a silver cup, silver play coins (several hundred if possible), a cloth bag for the coins, and a fabric bag (or a pillowcase) ready as props.

Illustrate Joseph's inspection of his brothers' sacks by opening your fabric bag 11 times to represent the 11 brothers. Shake your head no the first 10 times to show you didn't find the silver cup. As you open the bag the eleventh time, exclaim, **Here is the silver cup! I found it in Benjamin's sack!**

Tell how the brothers prepared to leave Egypt and return to Canaan to bring their father, Jacob, to live in Egypt. Hold up and count five sets of clothes (for example, five pairs of jeans and five T-shirts) to show the children the clothing Joseph gave Benjamin. Then show them a cloth bag. Pour out the silver play money to illustrate Joseph's gift. (Show 300 pieces of "silver" if possible.)

Emphasize God's loving care and protection for His servant, Joseph, and His forgiveness and the power to forgive others we have through Jesus Christ.

Tell about some times when we need God to help us show love and forgiveness.

a silver cup

cloth sack

pillowcase or fabric pouch

many silver play coins

God Takes Care of Baby Moses

Exodus 1:1–2:11

Bible words: God said, "I will be with you." *Exodus 3:12*

A Baby in a Basket

You will need a wicker or rattan basket, a doll wrapped in a lightweight blanket, an extra blanket, and a name card with *Moses* printed on it.

As you tell about Moses' birth, show the doll, and wrap it in the blanket. Allow your students to hold the doll as you tell how much Moses' mother, father, and sister loved him. Show your students the name card so they see the name *Moses*.

Show the basket and place the doll in it. Tell how Moses' mother could no longer hide him from the Egyptians. Explain that at three months old, Moses had begun to laugh and cry louder. His mother placed him in the basket to protect him from the soldiers. She had coated it with tar and pitch to make it waterproof. Place the other blanket over the basket. Pretend to carry it to the edge of the river. Rock the basket in your arms as you tell how it floated in the water.

Pretend to be the Pharaoh's daughter. Exclaim, **Oh! Look what I've found along the edge of the river! It's a baby boy! He is one of the Hebrew babies!** Uncover the doll in the basket.

Point out that God used the difficult times in Moses' life to make him a stronger person and to teach Moses to rely on God. God had a plan for Moses. He protected him and prepared him for the hard job he would face as the leader of God's people.

What are some difficult things you have had to do in your life? Whatever troubles we have, we can always trust God to help us face them and stay with us all the time.

The Passover

Exodus 12–13

Bible words: I am the Lord. *Exodus 12:12*

[God says,] "Do not fear, for I am with you; … I am your God." *Isaiah 41:10*

Celebrate the Feast of Unleavened Bread

As you tell the story of the Lord's Passover, explain that God spoke to Moses and Aaron in Egypt. He told them that on the tenth day of the month, each man should take a lamb for his family and take good care of it until the fourteenth day. On that evening, all the people should kill the lambs, spread the blood on the top and sides of their door frames, roast the meat over the fire, and eat it. (Draw a door and a door frame on poster board with permanent marker. Brush red tempera paint across this doorway as you describe the event.) Describe how the lamb symbolizes Jesus, the Lamb who was killed for our sins, the perfect Lamb sacrificed for all people.

Tell how God's people also were to eat bitter herbs—maror—with the roasted lamb to remind them of the bitter years of their slavery in Egypt. Freshly grated horseradish or onion remind us of the bitter suffering of the Israelites. (Give each child a piece of endive or chicory to taste.) These remind us that many people have suffered so that we may know the Good News of Jesus. In our celebration, we remember the great cost of our salvation: God's only Son.

The Israelites also ate unleavened bread—bread made without yeast—because God planned for them to leave Egypt quickly. This meant their bread would have no time to rise before baking. (Give each child a piece of matzoh to taste. If you cannot find matzoh in your grocery store or a delicatessen, hand out unsalted white crackers.) For Christians, this reminds us that we should be ready to go when Jesus returns.

The Lord told the people to burn any

leftovers. They were to eat quickly with their cloaks tucked into their belts (put a jacket on and tie a rope belt over it), their sandals on their feet (wear sandals or shoes), and with their staffs in their hands (hold a staff or a cane). These show they were in a hurry and ready to leave Egypt when God's time was right.

In Bible times, the Feast of Unleavened Bread began with the Passover meal and continued for seven days. Jewish families today begin their seven- or eight-day Passover observance with a meal and a family worship service they call "Seder" (or "Order") because they always keep the celebration in a certain order.

Other food items on the Seder table in the Christian home include a roasted egg or a hard-boiled egg in the shell, which represents God's ultimate gift of love for all people—Jesus, our Savior. Parsley or watercress, plants that stay green all year, represent God's gift of everlasting life because of Jesus' resurrection. Wine or grape juice represents joy. Jesus had to die so that we would know the total joy of freedom from sin and forgiveness through Him. In the center of the celebration table is Elijah's cup. This is a full goblet of wine to welcome Elijah and his announcement of the Messiah's coming. Christians share the cup of wine and rejoice that our Hope has already come and will come again on the last day. The Messiah—Christ—is alive and gives us eternal joy through Himself.

Emphasize that God kept His promise to save His people. He passed over the houses of the Israelites who had painted the lamb's blood on the door frame and then led them out of Egypt's slavery. He is with us today, and He promises that Jesus, our Savior, will come again.

God didn't forget His people. He doesn't forget us either. Tell about a time when you were in trouble or afraid. Did you remember to ask God for help? How did He help you?

God Provides Water for His People

Exodus 17:1–7

Bible words: You will know that I am the Lord your God. *Exodus 16:12*

A Long and Thirsty Walk

Collect a road map, a very large rock in a plastic dishpan, and a large pitcher of water. Also have a plastic or disposable cup for each student and teacher.

Show the road map as you tell about all of God's people—the Israelites—walking, crossing the desert, and camping from place to place. Tell how thirsty you become as you walk from one place to another for 40 years.

Use a grumbling voice as you tell how the people complained to Moses and questioned why the Lord had allowed them to leave Egypt.

Pretend to be Moses. Hold the wooden staff (or cane) and walk over to the large rock. Strike the rock with the staff. Arrange for a helper to pour the pitcher of water over the large rock when you hit it.

Remind your students that God gives us everything we need and that He is our loving God. Give them each a cup of water.

Talk about times when you have complained or grumbled about something. How can we let God know that we're sorry for our failure to trust Him?

Firstfruits for the Lord

Deuteronomy 26

Bible words: The Lord has declared this day that you are His people, His treasured possession. *Deuteronomy 26:18*

Offering Baskets

In this Bible story, we are reminded of God's command to the Israelites to give back to Him an offering of their best produce—the fruits from the land He gave them just as He had promised.

Gather a variety of baskets before class. Place a variety of the best fruit from the garden or market in one basket. Place the best vegetables from the garden or market in another basket. In a third basket, place coins and dollar bills as an offering.

As you tell the Bible story, place the baskets of fruit and vegetable offerings on the classroom altar. Say, **The Lord brought us out of Egypt with a mighty hand and an outstretched arm. He gave us this land flowing with milk and honey. Now we bring the firstfruits of the soil that He has given us.** Bow before the Lord.

Explain the practice of tithing (giving one-tenth of one's produce or income). Show your students 10 apples and count them together. Move one of the apples to the side and say, **This is one apple out of 10 apples. Let's say that my apple tree grew 10 beautiful apples. This one shiny apple would be my tithe to the Lord. I give back to Him my very best, reddest, shiniest apple as my way of thanking Him for all His good gifts to me.**

Remind students that after God's people gave Him one-tenth of their produce, they shared their fruits and vegetables with widows, orphans, and others in need.

Show the offering baskets or plates from your church or Sunday school classroom. Explain that when we place our offering in these containers, we give our money to Jesus as a thank-You. The money is used to buy Bibles and other Gospel materials so that more people can learn about Jesus and His forgiveness for them.

Give each child 10 dimes. Say, **Let's say I paid you 10 dimes for helping me rake leaves. Line up your 10 dimes. Now move one dime to the side. That one dime would be your tithe, the offering you would give to the Lord at church or Sunday school. When you give one-tenth of what you have, we call that tithing.**

Challenge your students to determine what their tithe to the Lord would be if they worked around their home and earned $2, $5, $10, and $100. Challenge them to set aside their tithe offerings for Jesus.

God Helps His People at the Battle of Jericho

Joshua 6

Bible words: [God says,] "Call upon Me in the day of trouble; I will deliver you, and you will honor Me." *Psalm 50:15*

Playact with Rhythm Instruments

Have your students build a large, tall wall using different-sized cardboard boxes.

Tell the story of Joshua leading God's people around the city of Jericho. March around your pretend city with your students seven times. The first six times, march without making noise. The seventh time around the "city," make noise with rhythm instruments, blow trumpets (or have everyone play a kazoo), and shout to announce the Lord's presence.

Knock over the wall as you shout and make noise.

To review the story, arrange the classroom to represent the battle setting. Ask students for their input and help in moving desks, chairs, and tables to designate the locations of Jericho and the Israelite camp.

Assign students to the parts of Joshua, the people of Jericho, Israelite soldiers, priests (some to carry the ark of the covenant; some to blow trumpets), and God's people who shout when Joshua gives the signal.

What are some ways that God shows His care and protection of you? Whom does God use to help you? Ask God to give you patience and to trust Him for love and care.

God Makes Samson Strong

Judges 13–16

Bible words: The Lord is my strength. *Psalm 28:7*

Playact with Dolls

You'll need six dolls for this Bible story—three men, two women, and a baby—to represent Manoah, his wife, the angel of God, and baby Samson. Dress the dolls in rectangles of fabric with yarn belts. Make two wigs of long hair for the adult Samson doll. (You can make these from strands of yarn glued, stitched, or taped together.) Tape one to the adult Samson doll's head. You'll use the second wig later in the story.

Show the angel with Manoah and his wife. Tell your students the angel's message and the command that Manoah and his wife should never cut Samson's hair. Describe the angel's ascension into heaven.

Place a small doll in the woman's arms. As you tell how Samson grew up and the blessings God gave him, remove the mother and father. Replace the baby Samson with the adult Samson doll with long hair.

Show Samson and Delilah talking together. Delilah should beg Samson repeatedly to tell her what makes him so strong. Each time Samson sleeps and the Philistines do what Delilah tells them, Samson should jump up as strong as ever.

Finally, Samson tires of her begging and tells Delilah the secret of his strength. Delilah talks to the Philistine rulers, the enemies. While Samson sleeps, an enemy cuts Samson's hair. Cut the yarn hair with your scissors.

Tell your students that Samson's hair had grown back. Place the second wig on Samson. The Philistine rulers brought Samson out of prison to watch him perform, and the temple was full of people. Place Samson between two large cardboard tubes (such as those in Christmas wrapping paper) to represent the large pillars of a building. Samson prayed to God for help. Then he pushed the pillars over, and Samson, the Philistine rulers, and all the people in the temple died. Place Samson lying down, dead along with the rulers and the people in the temple.

How did God help His servant Samson? What are some ways God helps you?

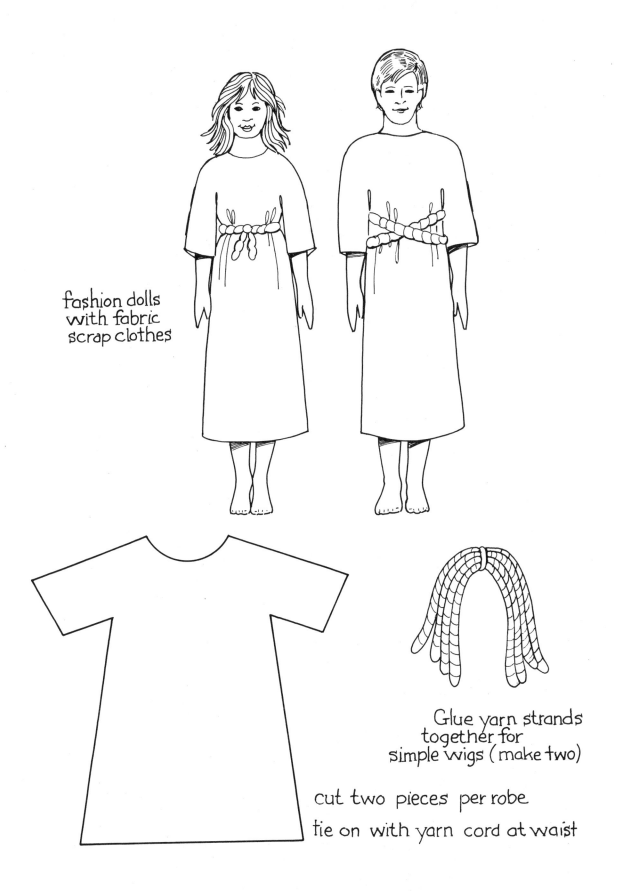

fashion dolls
with fabric
scrap clothes

Glue yarn strands
together for
simple wigs (make two)

cut two pieces per robe

tie on with yarn cord at waist

God Gives David Courage

1 Samuel 17

Bible words: The Lord be with you. *1 Samuel 17:37*

Life-Size Story Pictures

Use sturdy butcher paper to make your storytelling visuals. Cut life-size figures of Goliath (a man more than nine feet tall); David (a man about five and one-half feet tall); one or more sheep; a coat of armor; a bronze helmet; a sword; a wooden staff; five smooth stones; a shepherd's bag (pouch); and a leather sling. Add details to each of the visuals with tempera paint or permanent markers. Enlarge the illustrations on this page for patterns with an opaque projector.

Tape each visual to a wall as you tell the story of how God helped David and kept him safe against the enemy. Your students will see the contrast in size between the Philistine, Goliath, and David because of the life-size paper figures. Emphasize that God was with His servant, David, and kept him from any harm. David relied on his Lord, who gave him the strength and courage to face Goliath. God saved His people again, demonstrated His love for them, and showed His power to the world.

God has a job for you too. How can we know what our jobs are? How does God let us know what He wants us to do?

We can always trust that God is with us wherever we are and whatever we do.

Jonathan and David

1 Samuel 17:55–20:42

Bible words: [Jesus said,] "Love each other [one another] as I have loved you." *John 15:12*

Paperdoll Story Figures

Use the patterns to make paperdoll figures of David and Jonathan. Attach each paperdoll to a craft stick and place the stick in a lump of clay. Use a shoe box to represent the king's palace. Make a street outside the palace with Lego building blocks or other blocks. Use an oatmeal container to make a hiding place for David. Manipulate the paperdolls as you tell the story of the wonderful friendship God gave Jonathan and David.

Tell about a wonderful friend God has given to you. Why do you like your friend? How do you show love to your friend? Why is your friend a blessing in your life?

God Provides
for Elijah and the Widow

1 Kings 17

Bible words: The word of the Lord
... is the truth. *1 Kings 17:24*

Surprise Pictures

Look for pictures in old Sunday
school or vacation Bible school leaflets
that illustrate

- Elijah drinking from the brook;
- ravens bringing Elijah bread and meat
  near the brook where Elijah drank;
- a widow near a town gate, gathering
  sticks;
- a cake of bread;
- a jar of flour;
- a jug of oil;
- the widow's sick son;
- Elijah stretched out across the boy on
  his bed, praying;
- Elijah, the widow, and her son whom
  God had healed.

Crop each picture to show exactly
what you want your students to see as
you storytell. Tape the pictures in correct sequence to sturdy poster board.
Cover each picture completely with a dif-
ferent-colored piece of construction
paper. Tape the entire top of each piece

of construction paper to the poster
board. Hang the poster board on a bul-
letin board or a wall.

As you tell the Bible story, have your
students take turns lifting the pieces of
construction paper to reveal each story
visual. You might ring a bell or hum
"Jesus Loves Me, This I Know" as a signal to show the next picture.

If you don't have any old lesson
leaflets, make your own pictures. You
also could ask at a Christian bookstore
for visuals of the story of Elijah and the
widow.

During your presentation, you also
might show a clay container (a crock or
ceramic bowl) of flour, a jug of oil, and an
old-fashioned round of bread (or a biscuit).

Ask your students to retell the Bible
story to one another using the surprise
picture poster board for review.

Who are some people and what are
some things God has given to you to
take care of you? How do you feel knowing that you can trust God for everything that you need?

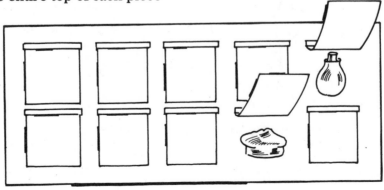

God's Helper, Isaiah

Isaiah 6

Bible words: "Here am I. Send me!" *Isaiah 6:8*

Cardboard Tube Figures

Gather empty cardboard tubes from toilet tissue, kitchen wrap, or Christmas wrapping paper. You'll need a tube to make Isaiah, a few for the seraphs, and a few for the people to whom Isaiah spoke.

Use fabric scraps, pieces of construction paper, aluminum foil, yarn, and any other "found" objects to make these story figures.

See Isaiah 6:2 for the description of the seraphs. Cut three sets of wings for each seraph. Use craft glue or a glue gun to attach one set of wings in the middle of the back. Attach a second set of wings a little higher on the back. Curve the wings around the front of the seraph and tape them together in front of the face. Attach the third set of wings a little lower on the back. Wrap them toward the front, taping them in front of the feet.

Cut a bright red circle of cellophane the size of a quarter. When a seraph flies to Isaiah with a live coal, tape the red cellophane to Isaiah's mouth.

Make the group of people—men, women, and children—to whom God sent Isaiah to prophesy.

God may not ever command a seraph to fly to us and place a live coal on our mouths. But God does call us to be His children and do His work. What work do you think God has for you to do? Would you like to become a missionary or a pastor or a teacher? How will you know what work He has for you as you grow up and become an adult? It is good to know that, whatever job God leads us to, we can share His love with the people around us. How do you feel knowing that God hears your prayers and answers them all in His way and in His time?

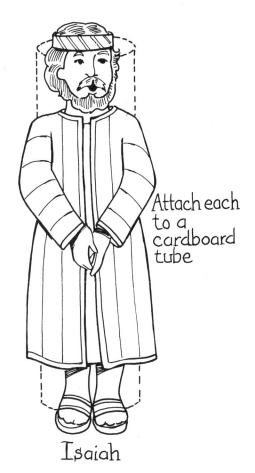

Attach each to a cardboard tube

Isaiah

angelic being
"seraph"

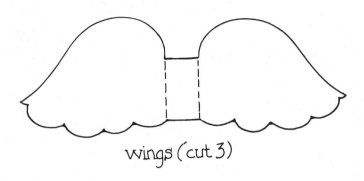

wings (cut 3)

cut a number of men and women

34

God Talks to Jeremiah

Jeremiah 1

Bible words: Go ... I send you ... I am with you. *Jeremiah 1:7–8*

Chenille Wire Figures

Prepare story figures for Jeremiah as a baby, a young boy, and an adult by bending chenille wires into the shapes of these figures. Cut faces from extra-fine sandpaper for each figure. Use a fine-point marker to add details. Glue the faces behind the chenille wire face outlines.

Also make chenille figures for the people to whom Jeremiah spoke.

Stand each chenille wire figure in a lump of clay or play dough. Or you can glue a small magnetic strip on the back of each figure. Then stick each figure to a cookie sheet or the side of a filing cabinet as you storytell.

What did God promise to His servant Jeremiah? Which of these promises are also true for me and you?

clay

Baby Jeremiah   young boy   adult
sandpaper faces

God Saves Daniel's Three Friends

Daniel 3

Bible words: Remember, I will be with you and protect you wherever you go. *Genesis 28:15* (TEV)

Finger Figures

Make finger figures using colorful construction paper, scissors, and a small stapler. Use red, yellow, and orange cellophane to represent the fiery furnace.

Use the basic pattern to create finger figures for King Nebuchadnezzar, Shadrach, Meshach, Abednego, and an angel.

Place King Nebuchadnezzar on the pointer finger of one hand.

Place Shadrach, Meshach, and Abednego on the first three fingers of your other hand.

Cover Shadrach, Meshach, and Abednego with layers of red, orange, and yellow cellophane to represent the fiery furnace.

Add the angel to your little finger. Wiggle all the figures "inside the fire."

Remove the angel figure. Then remove the cellophane. Move King Nebuchadnezzar close to Shadrach, Meshach, and Abednego as he tells them that their God is the true God.

Emphasize the courage these three men displayed in the face of danger and death. Only God could make them brave and save them. Discuss their strong faith and acceptance of God's will.

Would you be able to say no to someone in authority if that person told you to disobey God? How are your daily temptations different than the temptations Shadrach, Meshach, and Abednego experienced?

· roll paper into tube to fit your finger
· tape or staple strip of arms/hands
· add details with markers

Angel

King Nebuchadnezzar   Shadrach Meshach
Abednego

Jesus Is Born

Luke 1:26–38; 2:1–7

Bible words: [God] loved us and sent His Son. *1 John 4:10*

Christmas Story Gift Bag

Obtain a large, sturdy Christmas gift bag in a bright color. If possible, it should be decorated with stars, glitter, snowflakes, or other generic Christmas patterns but not with secular pictures such as Santa, reindeer, or snowmen. It may have an Advent or Christmas Bible story scene on it. It could be used as one of the storytelling visuals.

In the bag, place the following objects to pull out at the appropriate time in your storytelling.

- **An angel and a figure of Mary.** Cut a paper plate in half. Roll it into a cone shape. Tape or staple it so it stands by itself. Use scraps of lace, foil, wrapping paper, yarn for hair, and fine-point markers to add detail. The angel's mouth should be open as he talks to Mary. Give Mary a smile.

- **Joseph.** Staple together another half of a paper plate into a free-standing cone shape. Add facial features and scraps of fabric for clothing. Place Mary and Joseph in front of a shoebox house. Show them smiling.

- **A small blanket and a water jug.** Pull out a small blanket and a water jug from the gift bag as you tell about Mary and Joseph's long walk to Bethlehem.

- **An innkeeper.** Use half of a paper plate to make an innkeeper. Add details as you did for the other figures. Move the innkeeper back and forth as he tells Mary and Joseph there is no room in his inn. Move the innkeeper, Joseph, and Mary across the table as they follow him to the stable. Place a second shoebox on its side to represent the stable.

- **Baby Jesus.** Cut a small wedge from a paper plate. Fold and tape it in a small cone shape to make a baby. Add closed eyes and a smiling mouth.

- **A manger bed.** Pull out straw or hay (or strips of yellow construction paper) from your gift bag to represent the manger bed in which Mary placed baby Jesus.

What gift would make you the happiest boy or girl who ever lived? God gave us the best Christmas gift that was ever given—His Son, Jesus, our Savior. Why is Jesus our best gift of all? What are some ways God helps us "give" His gift of Jesus to people around us?

Angel

Mary

Baby Jesus

Joseph

gift bag

The Shepherds Worship Jesus

Luke 2:8–20

Bible words: Today … a Savior has been born to you. *Luke 2:11*

Follow the Footprints

Cut large footprint shapes from different colors of poster board.

On each footprint, draw a Bible story scene or character (or glue a picture from an old Sunday school or vacation Bible school leaflet). Begin at a far corner of your classroom and take "a story journey to Bethlehem." Plan to end at a location you have set up as a surprise stable scene. This could simply be a manger scene on a table at the end of the hallway. Or you could end up by the crèche in your church sanctuary or in front of the outdoor manger scene your church might display. At the final stop, plan to worship Jesus and praise Him with songs and a prayer.

Tell the Bible story in your own words, show the corresponding footprint visual, and have a student place it on the floor. As each element of the story is told, add another footprint. All the story footprints will lead you and your students on a journey to find the baby Jesus and worship Him as Savior and King.

You should include pictures of

- the angel's Good News to Mary;
- Mary and Joseph happy together;
- their long walk to Bethlehem;
- their stay in the innkeeper's stable;
- Jesus' birth in the stable.

In addition, show pictures of

- baby Jesus in His simple manger bed;
- a group of shepherds in the fields, watching their sheep at night;
- an angel speaking to the shepherds;
- a group of angels singing to the shepherds;
- the shepherds hurrying to Bethlehem;
- the shepherds worshiping baby Jesus in the stable.

Review the Bible story by singing the following words to the melody "Ten Little Indians."

> **One little, two little, three little shepherds,**
> **Four little, five little, six little shepherds,**
> **Seven little, eight little, nine little shepherds,**
> *** Run to find baby Jesus.**
> (For stanzas 2 and 3, sing these ending lines: *** Come to worship Jesus;**
> *** Go and tell of Jesus.**)

The shepherds were some of Jesus' first visitors. What do you think they thought and felt as they knelt to worship baby Jesus in the manger bed? On their way back to their sheep, what do you think the shepherds told people about the new Baby? What Good News has God given you to share with others?

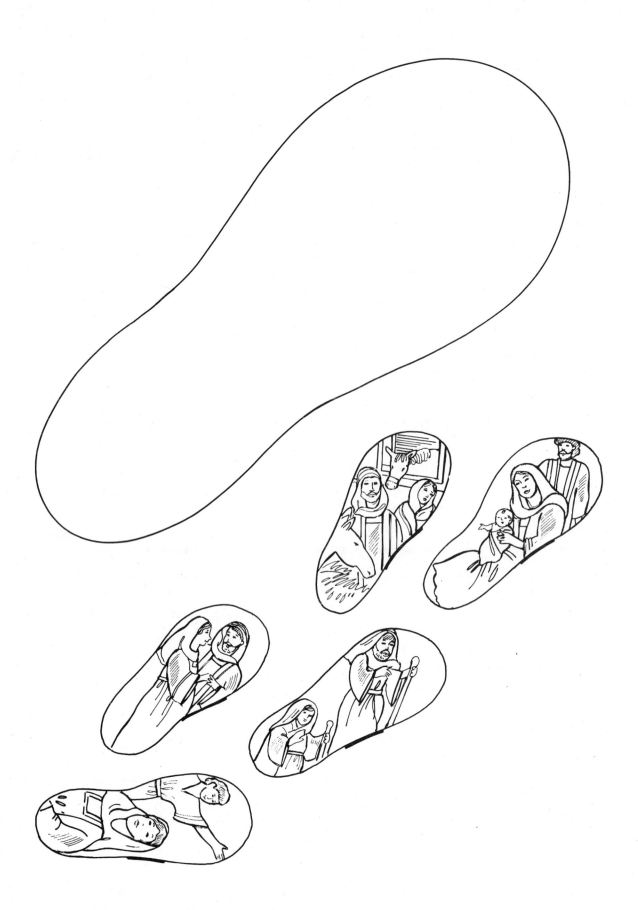

The Wise Men Worship Jesus

Matthew 2:1–12

Bible words: Come, let us bow down in worship. *Psalm 95:6*

Follow the Star

Begin by saying, **Let me tell you about some men who had waited a long time for God to send a special sign. This sign would show that God had sent the Savior—the King of the Jews. These men were the Magi or the Wise Men. The Wise Men knew that when they saw a special star in the sky, this would be a sign that the new King had been born.**

Continue telling the story from Matthew 2 in your own words. As you speak, slowly cut a large star from sturdy, shiny, gold or silver foil Christmas wrapping paper.

Begin with a sheet of paper 18″ x 24″ and a scissors. Fold the paper in half. Find the center of the top and the side. Label the points as shown.

Fold A from center B until it points to D.

Fold C down on line BD.

Fold BE to BD.

Cut through all the folds diagonally to make a five-pointed star.

You might cut in and out along all the edges to make a lacy star.

Tape the star above the manger scene in your classroom, or hang it above the manger with invisible fishing line.

Review the story by following the footprints discussed in the previous story. Have students retell the story of Jesus' birth, the shepherds hurrying to worship Jesus, and the Wise Men following the bright star to worship their new King.

The Wise Men followed the star so they could worship the new King and bring Him their gifts of gold, frankincense, and myrrh. What gifts has Jesus brought to us? What gifts can we give to Him?

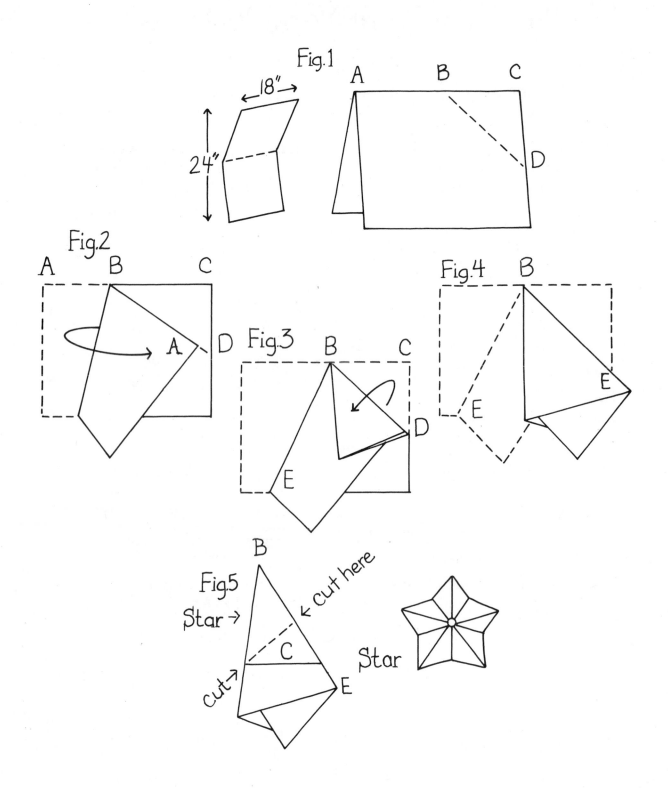

Fig.1

18″

24″

A   B   C

D

Fig.2

A   B   C

D

A

Fig.3   B   C

D

E

Fig.4   B

E

E

B

Fig.5
Star →

← cut here

C

cut →

E

Star

Jesus Calls His First Disciples

Matthew 4:18–22; Luke 6:12–19; John 1:35–51

Bible words: [Jesus said,] "Come, follow Me." *Matthew 4:19*

Clothesline and Clothespin Story

Attach a length of clothesline rope across a corner of your classroom or along a wall.

Use one clip clothespin to represent Jesus. Use a fine-point marker to draw facial features on the top of the clothespin. Tell about Jesus walking beside the Sea of Galilee as you clip the Jesus clothespin to the clothesline.

Use two clip clothespins for the brothers Simon (Peter) and Andrew. Draw their facial features with a fine-point marker. Clip them onto the clothesline. Clip a "fishing net" (a net vegetable bag) between them. You might place a couple of small plastic fish in the net as you tell about their job as fishermen.

Move Jesus close to Peter and Andrew as you tell about Jesus calling them to be His disciples. Take away the fishermen's net and fish. Show Peter and Andrew following Jesus.

Cut a fishing boat from poster board. Attach it to the clothesline. Clip three clothespin people into it: James, his brother, John, and their father, Zebedee. Clip a small portion of a fishing net to the side of their boat.

Move Jesus, Peter, and Andrew close to the fishing boat.

As you tell how Jesus called James and John to be His helpers, move James and John from the boat to the clothesline near Jesus.

Remove all the figures except Jesus. Attach a mountain cut from poster board to the clothesline. Tell about Jesus going to the mountain to pray and place Jesus near the mountain. Clothespin a few stars and a moon to the clothesline to represent night.

Remove the stars and moon. Clothespin a sun to the clothesline to represent day. Add one clothespin beside Jesus each time you name a disciple Jesus called: Simon Peter, Andrew, James, John, Philip, Bartholomew, Matthew, Thomas, James—son of Alphaeus, Simon the Zealot, Judas—son of James, and Judas Iscariot (who became a traitor).

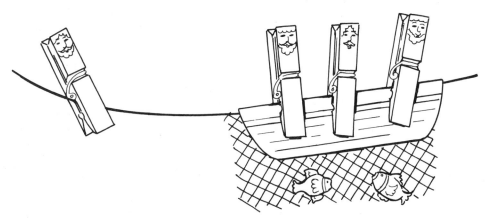

Jesus Changes Water into Wine

John 2:1–11

Bible words: I will be glad and rejoice in You. Psalm 9:2

Celebration Time

Gather Styrofoam egg cartons (as many as your table can hold). Prepare 12 plastic spoons or Sporks for every egg carton. On one side of each spoon, use a permanent marker to draw a sad face. On the opposite side of each spoon, draw a happy face. These represent the people at the wedding reception. Use a knife to make a slit in the bottom of each egg cup. Insert a plastic spoon into each slit.

As you tell the story and describe the celebration, point out the happy faces of all the wedding guests as they enjoy the party. Turn the cartons so the guests' sad faces show to represent their sadness because the bridegroom ran out of wine.

Beside the egg cartons full of guests, place seven clean, clear plastic jars (such as those peanut butter comes in). Six of the jars should be empty. In the seventh jar, put a package of grape or cherry drink mix. Fill the six empty jars with water when Jesus tells the servants to fill the clay jars with water.

As you tell about Jesus asking the servants to draw water from the jars and take some to the master of the banquet, pour water from one of the six jars into the seventh. Exclaim over the miracle that Jesus performed at this wedding, turning water into wine.

Now show the happy faces of the guests Jesus helped make happy again.

Use a red permanent marker to draw hearts on some of the spoons to remind us that Jesus' disciples put their faith in Him.

Jesus Heals a Paralyzed Man

Mark 2:1–12; Luke 5:17–26

Bible words: [Jesus said,] "If you believe, you will receive whatever you ask for in prayer." *Matthew 21:22*

[Jesus said,] "Friend, your sins are forgiven." *Luke 5:20*

Clothespin People

Use a medium-size cardboard box to represent a house.

Make Bible people from round-headed clothespins. Use clay or play dough as bases for the clothespin people. Make facial expressions directly on the wooden heads with fine-point markers. You also can cover a small amount of quilt batting or a cotton ball with a square of nylon hosiery for each figure's head. Secure this head to the top of the clothespin with a rubber band. Use a fine-point marker to make facial features.

Make clothing from fabric scraps and yarn. Use scraps of wood or cardboard to make the bed for the paralyzed man.

Tell the Bible story using the visuals at the appropriate times.

Emphasize that Jesus has the power to forgive sins and to heal sicknesses.

Have your students manipulate the clothespin people as they retell the Bible story.

What do you believe that Jesus has done for you? What do you trust Jesus to do for you each day? When we believe that Jesus is our Savior and friend, what does the Holy Spirit help us do each day?

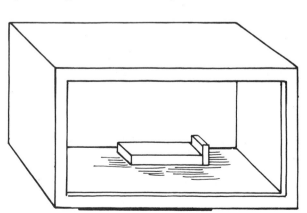

Jesus Heals a Centurion's Servant

Matthew 8:5–13; Luke 7:1–10

Bible words: [Jesus says,] "If you believe, you will receive whatever you ask for in prayer." *Matthew 21:22*

Tube Puppets

Before class, prepare a set of tube puppets using nine cardboard tubes and the patterns on page 47. Toilet tissue tubes work well. Color the puppets with markers or crayons, cut them out, and glue each to a tube. Make the sad servant without a tube so you can place it flat. The happy servant can be glued to a tube to show he can stand.

Use a table or desk as a stage so students can see as you tell the Bible story. Introduce each puppet as it appears in the story.

Emphasize the centurion's strong faith and Jesus' miracle. Remind your students that God gave the centurion the faith that he had. Apply the Bible lesson by sharing this story about faith.

Hide an unshelled peanut in your closed hand.

I have something in my hand that is very special. You and I have never seen it before. You and I will never see it again. Raise your hand if you believe that I have something like that in my hand. (Some might not raise their hands.)

I'm your teacher, and I tell you God's true words. I'm telling you the truth. Raise your hand if you believe that I have something in my hand that we've never seen before, and we'll never see again. (You may still have doubters.)

Shell the peanut in front of your students. Show everyone what you have. **Look! This is something you and I have never seen before. It was hidden inside its shell.**

Eat the peanut. **Now you and I will never see it again! Raise your hand if you believe what I said in the beginning—that I had something in my hand that you and I have never seen before, and we will never see it again!**

Help your students understand that faith is not seeing but accepting you at your word.

We can't see God, can we? We couldn't see the peanut. But we believe God and His Word. We know He is with us and loves us all the time. We have faith in Him.

We weren't there when Jesus died on the cross. But we believe God's Word, the Bible, when we read that "God loved the world so much that He gave His one and only Son." We have faith in Jesus and His forgiveness.

When the centurion sent the church leaders to meet Jesus, he had faith that Jesus could and would make his servant well.

Jesus—only Jesus—has the power to forgive and heal people. He answers our prayers according to what He knows is best for us. God gives us His forgiveness and love through Jesus.

centurion

friend

Jesus

friend

servant

friend

church leader

friend

church leader

servant

47

The Parable of the Sower

Luke 8:1–15

Bible words: The seed is the word of God. *Luke 8:11*

A Parable Table

Set up a "parable table" (a learning center) in your classroom. At the table your students can touch and hold objects that relate to the Bible lesson.

For this Bible story, you'll want

- a packet of seeds (lettuce seed or marigold seed);
- seeds in a closed baby food jar, easy for students to see;
- a foil cake pan with a few inches of soil in the bottom;
- birds from a craft store;
- a foil cake pan with a little soil and many rocks and stones;
- a foil cake pan with a little soil and plants that represent thorns (or thorny twigs);
- a foil cake pan with a few inches of potting soil;
- a watering can or a spray misting bottle.

Show each item as you tell the parable that Jesus told to His followers.

Scatter a small amount of seed on each of the types of ground: the trampled ground, the rocky area, the thorny patch, and the good soil.

Have your students take turns spraying water on the seeds in the pans. Keep the quick-growing seeds in a sunny window and watch their growth in the good soil.

Remind your students that the seeds in the good soil are like the people with "noble and good hearts" who hear God's Word, remember it, and live their God-given faith.

The Parable of the Lost Sheep

Luke 15:3–7

Bible words: Rejoice with me; I have found my lost sheep. *Luke 15:6*

A Sheep Hunt

Before class, cut 100 sheep from construction paper or poster board. Outline the figures and add features with black permanent marker. Glue cotton batting to the sheep figures to provide extra sensory stimulation for your students.

Save them in a box or a large storage envelope for future use.

Before you begin the parable, hide one sheep in your classroom (without your students noticing). Place the other 99 sheep on the parable table (or learning center table).

Have your students gather around the table. Count the sheep together as you begin the story. **What? We're missing one of our sheep? That's terrible news! We must find it right away!**

Talk about how sad and worried the shepherd is when he loses one of his sheep. Tell how a sheep or a lamb might be hurt or killed by a wolf or another predator. Go on a "sheep hunt" with your students, looking for that one lost sheep. When someone finds it, clap and thank him or her. Show your happiness that the lost sheep has been found.

Ask your students if they have ever been lost from their parents or if they have ever lost a dog or cat. Allow them to tell how they felt when they or their pet was lost and then found again.

Explain that all God's angels rejoice and celebrate loudly in heaven when one sinner who "is lost" says he or she is sorry for his or her sins. We can celebrate the forgiveness and love that Jesus has given us through His death and resurrection. We need not be "a lost sheep," rather we are God's children—His saved lambs—in His family.

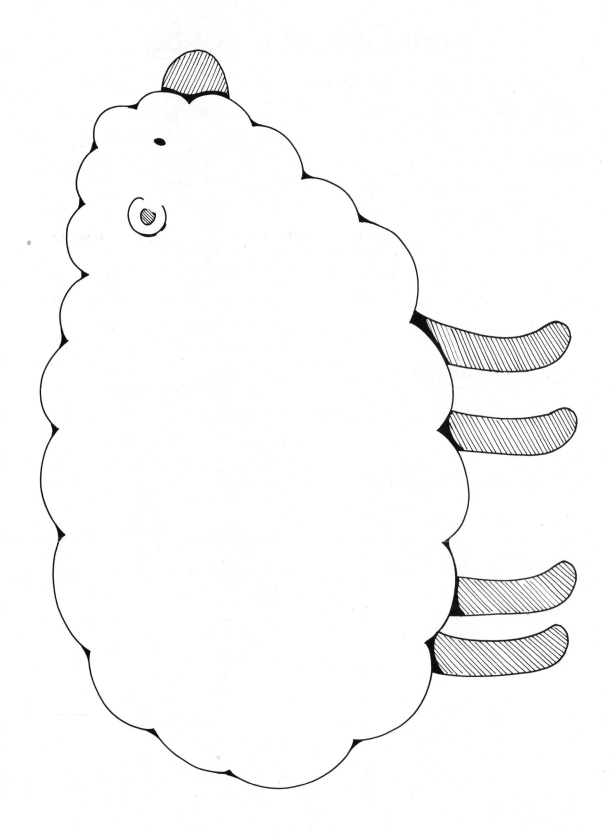

Jesus Calms the Storm

Matthew 8:23–27; Mark 4:35–41; Luke 8:22–25

Bible words: "I am with you always." Matthew 28:20

Wave Bottles

Before class, prepare a wave bottle for each student. You'll need to save clear plastic bottles from soda (one- or two-liter bottles), bottled water, or vegetable oil.

For each wave bottle, do the following:

Remove the label.

Fill the bottle ¼ full with generic vegetable oil.

Mix a drop of blue food coloring into one cup of water. Add this to the oil in the bottle.

Close the bottle tightly and seal it with plastic tape or duct tape.

Have your students turn their bottles on their sides and move them to make waves as you tell how the wind and the waves got stronger and higher when the disciples were in the boat with Jesus.

Ask your students if they have ever been at the lake or on a boat in the middle of a storm. Allow them to tell how afraid they were and who helped them.

Remind your students that we can ask Jesus to help us at all times. We can trust Him to take good care of us, just as He protected His helpers long ago. Jesus has all power over the wind and the waves.

The Forgiving Father

Luke 15:11–32

Bible words: Your heavenly Father will also forgive you. Matthew 6:14

God Washes Us Clean

After you tell the parable, emphasize the forgiveness and open arms of the waiting earthly father, who missed his son and welcomed him home with great celebration.

Our heavenly Father welcomes us back to Him after we have disobeyed and repented of our wrongdoing. Our heavenly Father washes away our sin through the saving actions of His Son, Jesus, our Savior, and remembers our sin no more.

Demonstrate how God erases our sin forever by showing your students this simple experiment.

Pour red food coloring into a large, clear glass of water. The red represents our sinful selves.

Pour chlorine bleach from another glass into the glass of red water. The water becomes clear immediately. Let that "washing" represent God's forgiveness through Jesus. He washes us clean completely. He forgives and forgets our sins.

Jesus Feeds the 5,000

Matthew 14:14–21; Mark 6:30–44; Luke 9:10–17; John 6:1–15

Bible words: Give thanks to the Lord, for He is good. Psalm 106:1

Baskets of Food

Before class, place five small loaves of bread (dollar rolls or small loaves from a discount bakery) and two plastic fish (from a child's play food set) into a small basket.

Gather 12 wicker baskets or picnic baskets (or use 12 small laundry baskets). You might borrow any of these from friends and neighbors or find them at garage sales and flea markets.

Place the "leftover food" in the 12 baskets. You might use bags of stale bread from discount stores and fish cut from different colors of poster board.

Show these items at the appropriate times during your storytelling.

Emphasize that Jesus supplies us with everything we need to live. He is our true Bread of Life because He has come from heaven to give us eternal life.

Jesus Heals 10 Men

Luke 17:11–19

Bible words: [Jesus said,] "Your faith has made you well." Luke 17:19

Story Gloves

Before class, prepare two canvas gloves (work gloves or gardening gloves) to serve as storytelling visuals.

Lay the gloves with the palms facing upward. Use a glue gun to attach a large pom-pom to the top of each finger and each thumb. Glue small wiggle eyes to each pom-pom. Glue a short piece of yarn on each pom-pom to make a frown. Use a red permanent marker to make leprosy spots on each finger and thumb. (Make spots only on the palm sides).

Turn the gloves over so that the thumbs are side by side. Glue a second set of small wiggle eyes to each pom-pom. Glue a short piece of yarn on each pom-pom to make a smile. Use a green permanent marker to draw a heart on one index finger to identify the one man who thanked Jesus for healing him and to symbolize the faith God gave him.

Show the 10 men with leprosy by holding your gloved hands with the palm sides facing your students. Wiggle the fingers and thumbs when the men cry, "Jesus, Master, have pity on us!"

When Jesus heals the leprous men, turn the gloves around to show the happy faces and spotless bodies.

Wiggle all your fingers and thumbs as you tell that they did what Jesus said and ran to show themselves to the priests.

Bend down all the fingers and thumbs except for the index finger that represents the one thankful man. Show the thankful man wiggling and jumping for joy, praising God in a loud voice.

Emphasize to your students that this one thankful man, a Samaritan, received not only the physical healing but also a spiritual healing and the gift of salvation. Point to the green heart on his body to represent a growing faith in this person.

When we ask Jesus in prayer to heal us or someone we love, we can trust that He will do what is best for the sick person. Jesus gives us exactly what we need—His love, His forgiveness, special helpers on earth, and the courage and strength we need. Sometimes His answer might be "no" or "I have other plans for you." Then He comforts us and reminds us that He knows what is best for us.

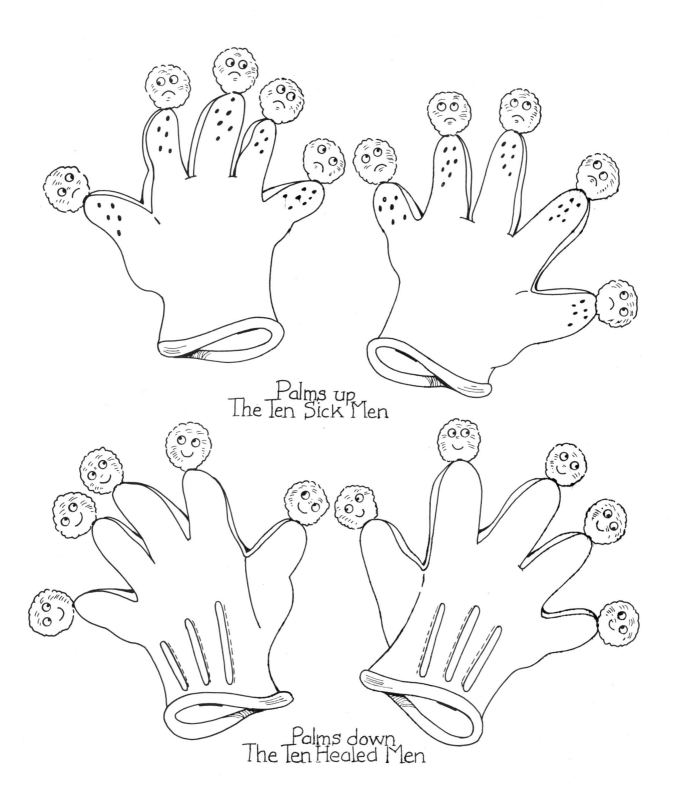

Palms up
The Ten Sick Men

Palms down
The Ten Healed Men

Jesus Heals a Blind Man

Mark 10:46–52; Luke 18:35–43

Bible words: [Jesus says,] "I am the light of the world." John 8:12

Coins in a Cup

Tell this Bible story from the first-person perspective. Practice telling the story in your own words before class. Put on an oversize shirt or robe, cover your head with a cloth and headband, and hold a metal cup for a beggar's cup. Have pennies ready for you and your students to drop into the cup. Sit on a carpet square and have your students sit in a semicircle in front of you.

Hello, girls and boys. My name is Bartimaeus. Not long ago I was a blind man. I couldn't run like you do. When I tried to run, I bumped into everything and got hurt. I couldn't work, either, because I couldn't see. No one would hire me. So I brought my begging cup and sat on this corner every day. Some people dropped coins into my cup. (Drop a few coins into your cup.) Then I could buy wheat and corn to make my food.

One day while I sat on the corner begging, I heard a crowd of people walking by. Someone told me it was Jesus. I had heard about Jesus. I believed He was the Savior and King that God had sent to the world to save all people. I believed that Jesus was MY Savior. I called out, "Jesus! Have mercy on me!"

The crowd of people told me to be quiet and not to bother Jesus. But I called out again anyway, "Jesus! Have mercy on me!"

Jesus heard me. He called me to come to Him. People helped me get up and walk to Jesus. He asked me what I wanted Him to do. I answered, "I want to see again."

Jesus told me, "You will see. Your faith has made you well!"

I could see Jesus' kind face right away! I could see my Savior! I could see the blue sky and the green grass. I could see all the surprised faces of the people around us. I was so happy!

I thanked Jesus. Then I followed Him down the road as He walked on to Jerusalem.

Have your students drop their coins into Bartimaeus' cup and take turns telling a part of the story to review the story.

How did Jesus give the blind Bartimaeus light? physically? spiritually?

How can Jesus be our Light when we play together? when we sin against someone? when someone hurts us?

How has Jesus helped you find your way by being your special light?

Jesus Rides into Jerusalem

Matthew 21:1–11; Mark 11:1–11; Luke 19:29–40; John 12:12–19

Bible words: Blessed is the king who comes in the name of the Lord! Luke 19:38

Chalk Tray Visuals and Emerald Fronds

A few weeks ahead of time, order inexpensive emerald fronds from a florist. You'll need one for each student during this storytelling presentation. Emerald fronds are the green, palm-like, "filler" greenery that go into floral arrangements. Though they aren't very sturdy, they serve well as small, temporary replicas of palm branches for students to wave in the classroom.

Prepare the following visuals (laminate them if possible) to represent the people and items in the story. Have your students place their coats or sweaters on the backs of their chairs to use as they participate in the story.

Place each visual along the chalk tray as you tell the Bible story. Point to the picture and to the word so that your students can visualize what you are telling them. Look through old Sunday school or vacation Bible school leaflets to find the pictures listed below.

- **Jesus**—A picture of a standing Jesus.
- **Jerusalem**—An outline of a city drawn on a piece of gray construction paper; print *Jerusalem* on it.
- **Mount of Olives**—A green hill cut from construction paper; print *Mount of Olives* on it.
- **A small donkey**—A picture of a donkey; print *donkey* on it.
- **Jesus on the donkey**—A picture of Jesus riding the donkey into Jerusalem.

At this point, ask your students to stand and pretend to be the crowds of people lining the streets of Jerusalem. Tell them to place their coats and sweaters on the floor and wave the emerald fronds (or green paper palm branches cut from construction paper) as you say, **Blessed is the king who comes in the name of the Lord!**

Have you ever watched a parade and seen important people coming through your town or city? How did you feel? What did you do and say?

Jesus, our King, promises to come again. Will you be ready for Jesus? What will you do and say then?

How might we welcome our Savior and King into our lives each morning and remember what He has done for us?

Mount of Olives

Jerusalem

donkey

Jesus Died for All People/ Jesus Is Alive

Matthew 27:11–28:15; Mark 16:1–13; Luke 24:1–49; John 20:1–18

Bible words: He died for all. 2 Corinthians 5:15

[Jesus] died for us so that, … we may live together with Him. *1 Thessalonians 5:10*

[Jesus said,] "Because I live, you also will live." *John 14:19*

A Diorama

Before class, make a diorama—a scene inside a box—to use as a visual to tell the Bible story.

Use a large cardboard box with the sides cut down. (Or use a large Rubbermaid under-the-bed storage box with a lid.)

Fill the box with clean sand, pea gravel, or cornmeal. Make the city of Jerusalem at one end of the box by placing small boxes side by side for houses. Boxes from deodorants, cosmetics, and other small products work well. Make a city wall by cutting a strip of poster board and placing it in the sand.

Make a hill outside the city wall by turning a bowl upside down. Make a tomb in a hillside by placing a small bowl on its side in the sand. Cut a "stone" from cardboard or poster board to place in front of the open grave. You also can use the lid of the bowl covered with construction paper to make it look like a large stone. Place a few trees (twigs and small leafy branches) in the valleys.

Use craft sticks for the Bible story characters. Use a fine-point marker to make facial features. Glue on fabric or scrap paper for clothing. Make wooden crosses from Lincoln Logs. Use rubber bands to secure the figures of Jesus and the two robbers to the crosses.

Place the craft-stick people that represent Jesus' disciples, Peter and John, and the women in bases made of clay or play dough. Move the characters as you tell the story.

Review the actions Jesus did for all people. What promises can we trust Jesus to keep for us?

Jesus Ascends into Heaven

Luke 24:50–53; Acts 1:1–11

Bible words: [Jesus says,] "I am with you always." Matthew 28:20

A Silhouette Story

Before class, set up an overhead projector and prepare story figures for the visuals. Practice telling the story as you move the paper visuals on the projector.

From dark construction paper, cut 11 figures to represent Jesus' disciples.

Cut a figure with His arms outstretched to represent Jesus.

Cut a cloud shape large enough to completely cover Jesus.

Cut two figures from waxed paper to represent the angels who stood by the disciples after Jesus rose into the clouds. Add facial details with a fine-point marker.

Use a permanent black marker to draw a smile on a piece of yellow cellophane shaped like a face.

As you tell the story, place the 11 disciples on the projector. Have your students count with you as you place each figure.

Place Jesus beside His 11 helpers, as though He were standing right next to them.

Very slowly, move Jesus upward as you tell how He rose into the sky. At the same time, move the cloud over Him to show that a cloud hid Him from the disciples' sight.

Place the two angels beside the disciples as you tell their promising message to Jesus' friends.

Remove the story figures you have used so far.

Place the happy, bright face on the projector as you apply the story to your students' lives.

Remind your students that Jesus promises to always be with them, to come again, and to take all who believe in Him to live with Him in heaven someday. Encourage them to tell someone this Good News, to pray for people who don't know Jesus as their Savior and friend, and to ask the Holy Spirit to help them tell others about Jesus and His love.

The First Pentecost

Acts 2:1–47

Bible words: "You will receive power when the Holy Spirit comes on you." Acts 1:8

Balloon People

Make 12 balloon people to represent Jesus' helpers as you tell this Bible story. (Matthias was added to the 11 disciples to replace Judas.)

Blow up 12 large red balloons before class and tie them closed.

Use a permanent marker to give each balloon eyes and an open mouth to show surprise. Draw a beard on one balloon to represent Peter.

Cut a set of feet from poster board for each of the disciples. Pull the knotted end of the balloon through a slit in the center of the feet piece so that each helper stands. Place a piece of double-sided tape on the bottom of each feet piece to anchor the balloon people to the table.

Cut an orange flame from construction paper for each of the balloon heads. Have clear tape ready to attach the flames to Jesus' helpers.

As you tell the Bible story, place all the balloon people together on a table to show they were gathered in one place. Make sure they are secured to the table with tape.

Make a whooshing sound to represent the sound of a blowing violent wind—the presence of the Holy Spirit.

Tape a paper flame to the top of each of the disciple's heads to represent the appearance of the Holy Spirit.

Move Peter in front of the 11 helpers to speak to the crowd of people.

Emphasize to your students that God gives two gifts—the forgiveness of sins and the Holy Spirit. The Spirit appeared as bright flames of fire on the first Pentecost. Fire and the color red reminds us of the Spirit's power to create faith in our hearts. Show your students the following experiment that relates to the Holy Spirit's work in our lives.

The Spirit Lives in Us

Fill two clear glasses with water. Add two teaspoons of white vinegar and two teaspoons of sugar to one glass. Both glasses of water will appear clear. Tell your students that only God knows what's in our hearts and minds. Drop a little baking soda into the plain water. It will sink. Drop a pinch of baking soda into the other glass. It will bubble and may overflow.

Relate this to the Holy Spirit's action in our lives. The Holy Spirit comes to us in our Baptism, in the Lord's Supper, and in God's Word. He lives in us. God's love and His power for us are bubbling over!

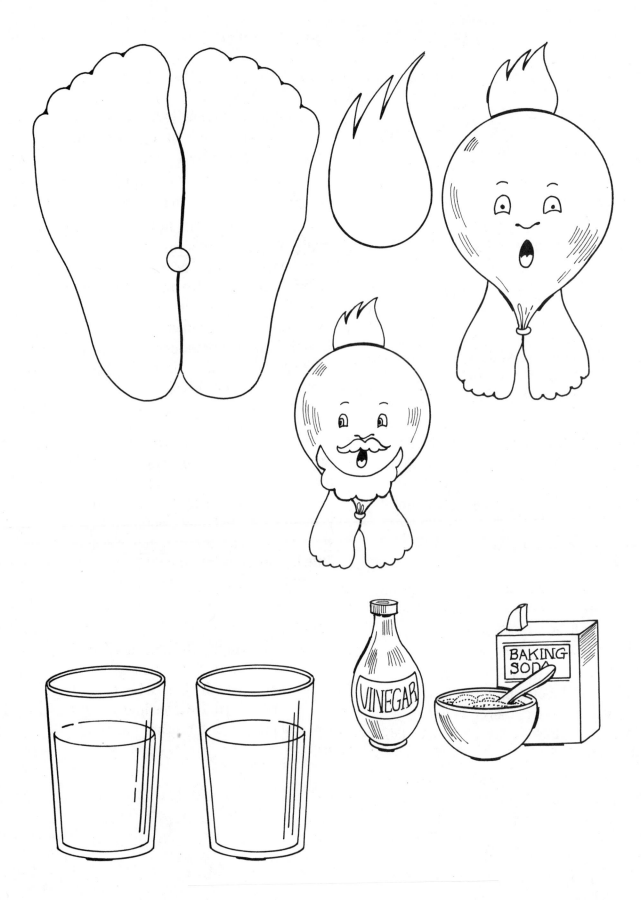